JAN 1 5

JR. GRAPHIC GHOST STORIES

SLEEPY HOLLOW

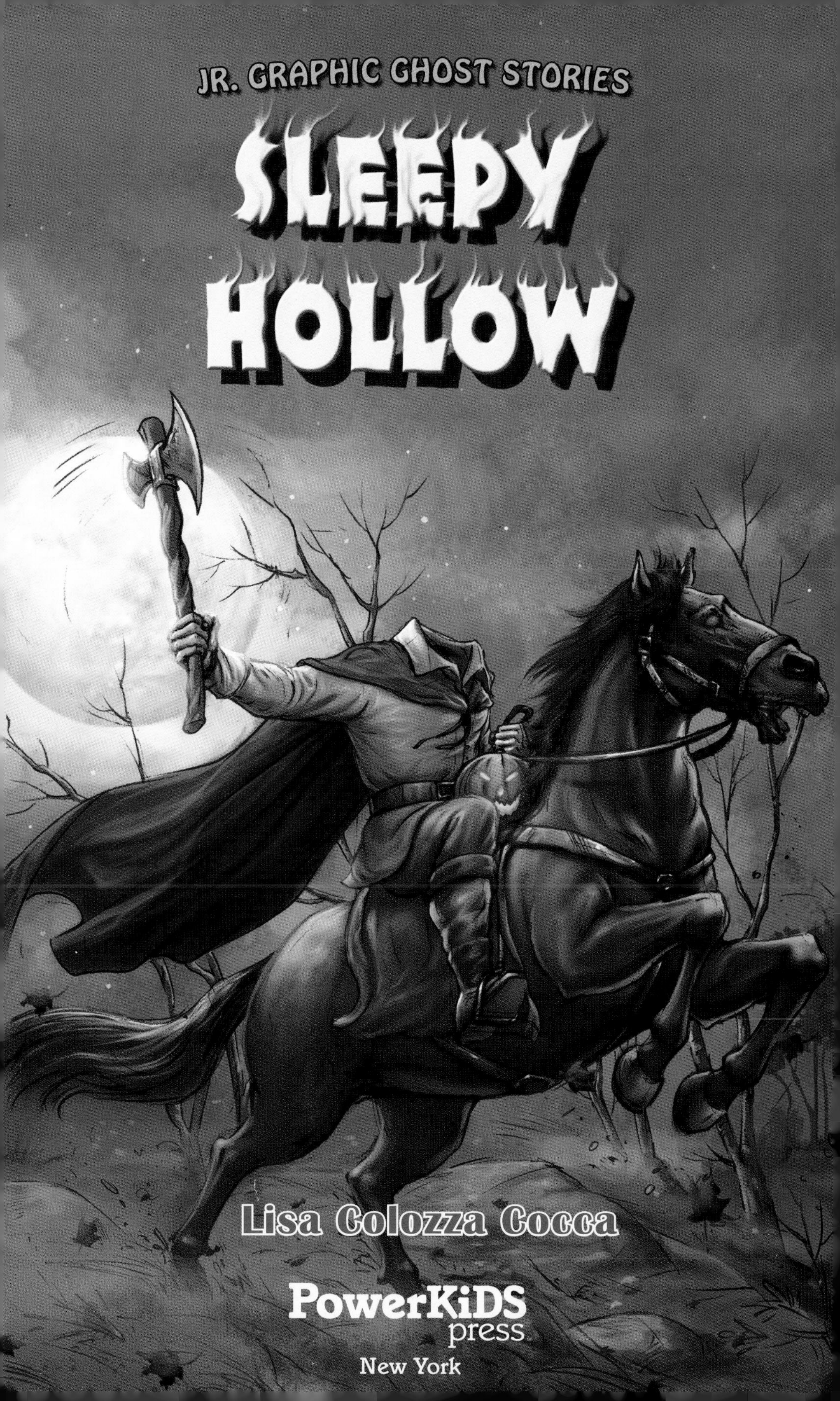

Lisa Colozza Cocca

PowerKiDS press.
New York

Published in 2015 by The Rosen Publishing Group, Inc.
29 East 21st Street, New York, NY 10010

First Edition

Editor: Joanne Randolph
Book Design: Contentra Technologies
Illustrations: Contentra Technologies

Publisher's Cataloging Data

Cocca, Lisa Colozza.
Sleepy Hollow / by Lisa Colozza Cocca — first edition.
p. cm. — (Jr. graphic ghost stories)
Includes index.
ISBN 978-1-4777-7084-9 (library binding) — ISBN 978-1-4777-7085-6 (pbk.) — ISBN 978-1-4777-7086-3 (6-pack)
1. Folklore — United States — Juvenile literature. 2. Folklore — Juvenile literature. I. Cocca, Lisa Colozza, 1957–. II. Title.
GR105.C63 2015
398—d23

Manufactured in the United States of America

CPSIA Compliance Information: Batch #WS14PK2: For Further Information contact Rosen Publishing, New York, New York at 1-800-237-9932

Contents

Introduction   3

Main Characters   3

The Legend of Sleepy Hollow   4

More Ghost Stories   22

Glossary   23

Index and Websites   24

Introduction

"The **Legend** of Sleepy Hollow," written by Washington Irving, was first published in 1819. This was about 26 years after the end of the American Revolution. Many small battles had been fought around Sleepy Hollow, a village in New York along the Hudson River, during the war. When the war ended, the people in the area told many stories about a headless horseman. The rider was said to be the ghost of a **Hessian** soldier who had lost his head in a battle against the Colonial forces. This soldier rode through the hollow at high speeds, chasing all other riders away. Irving's "The Legend of Sleepy Hollow" is based on the tale of the headless Hessian soldier.

Main Characters

Ichabod Crane A native of Connecticut who came to Sleepy Hollow to teach and also became the town's **singing master**.

Brom Bones The local hero, Bones was big, strong, and skilled on a horse.

The Headless Horseman The ghost of a Hessian soldier who lost his head in battle.

Old Baltus van Tassel The richest farmer in the area, well-known for his hospitality and for his lovely daughter, Katrina.

Katrina van Tassel The daughter of a wealthy farmer.

The Legend of Sleepy Hollow

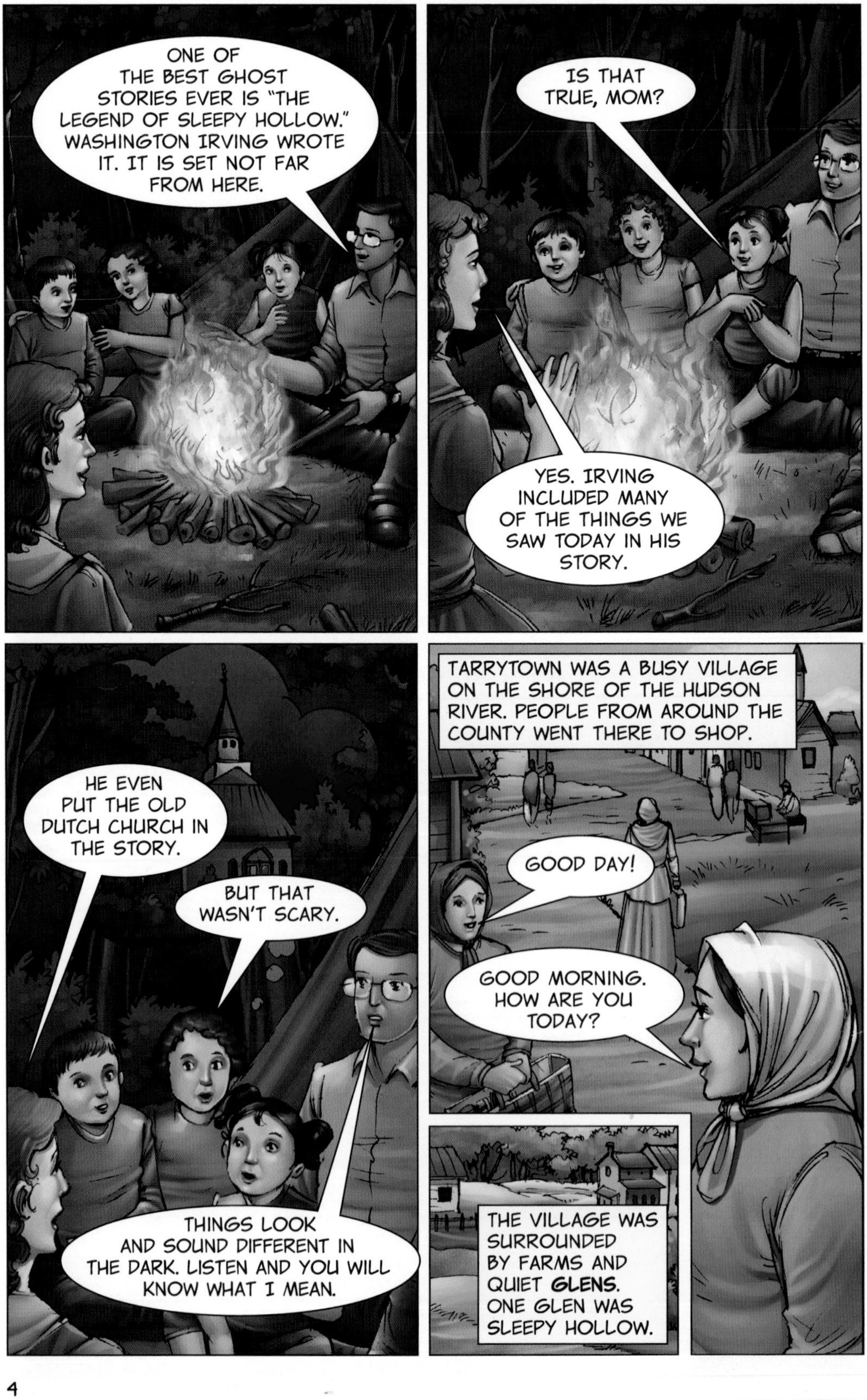

ONE OF THE BEST GHOST STORIES EVER IS "THE LEGEND OF SLEEPY HOLLOW." WASHINGTON IRVING WROTE IT. IT IS SET NOT FAR FROM HERE.
IS THAT TRUE, MOM?
YES. IRVING INCLUDED MANY OF THE THINGS WE SAW TODAY IN HIS STORY.
HE EVEN PUT THE OLD DUTCH CHURCH IN THE STORY.
BUT THAT WASN'T SCARY.
THINGS LOOK AND SOUND DIFFERENT IN THE DARK. LISTEN AND YOU WILL KNOW WHAT I MEAN.
TARRYTOWN WAS A BUSY VILLAGE ON THE SHORE OF THE HUDSON RIVER. PEOPLE FROM AROUND THE COUNTY WENT THERE TO SHOP.
GOOD DAY!
GOOD MORNING. HOW ARE YOU TODAY?
THE VILLAGE WAS SURROUNDED BY FARMS AND QUIET **GLENS**. ONE GLEN WAS SLEEPY HOLLOW.

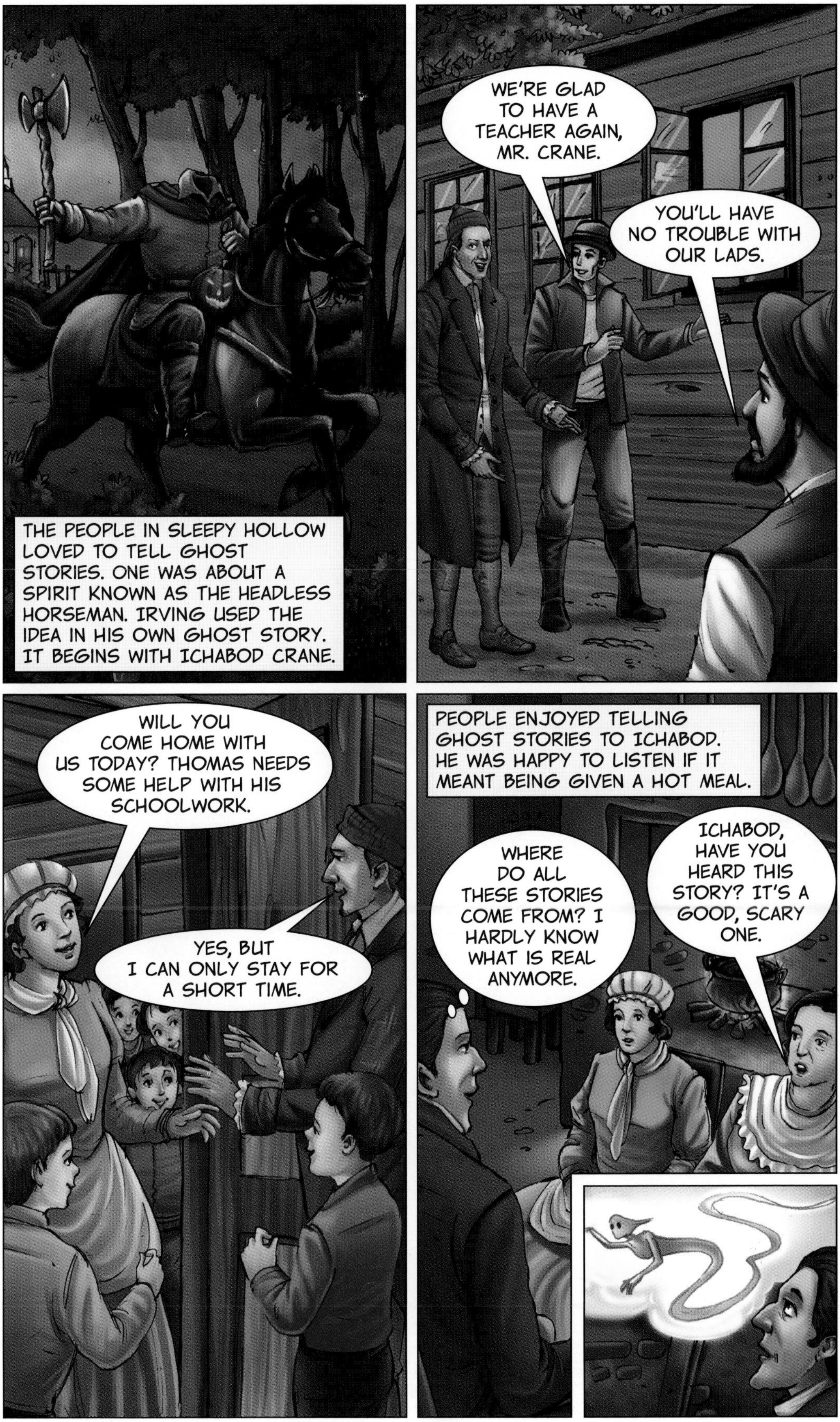

THE PEOPLE IN SLEEPY HOLLOW LOVED TO TELL GHOST STORIES. ONE WAS ABOUT A SPIRIT KNOWN AS THE HEADLESS HORSEMAN. IRVING USED THE IDEA IN HIS OWN GHOST STORY. IT BEGINS WITH ICHABOD CRANE.
WE'RE GLAD TO HAVE A TEACHER AGAIN, MR. CRANE.
YOU'LL HAVE NO TROUBLE WITH OUR LADS.
WILL YOU COME HOME WITH US TODAY? THOMAS NEEDS SOME HELP WITH HIS SCHOOLWORK.
YES, BUT I CAN ONLY STAY FOR A SHORT TIME.
PEOPLE ENJOYED TELLING GHOST STORIES TO ICHABOD. HE WAS HAPPY TO LISTEN IF IT MEANT BEING GIVEN A HOT MEAL.
ICHABOD, HAVE YOU HEARD THIS STORY? IT'S A GOOD, SCARY ONE.
WHERE DO ALL THESE STORIES COME FROM? I HARDLY KNOW WHAT IS REAL ANYMORE.

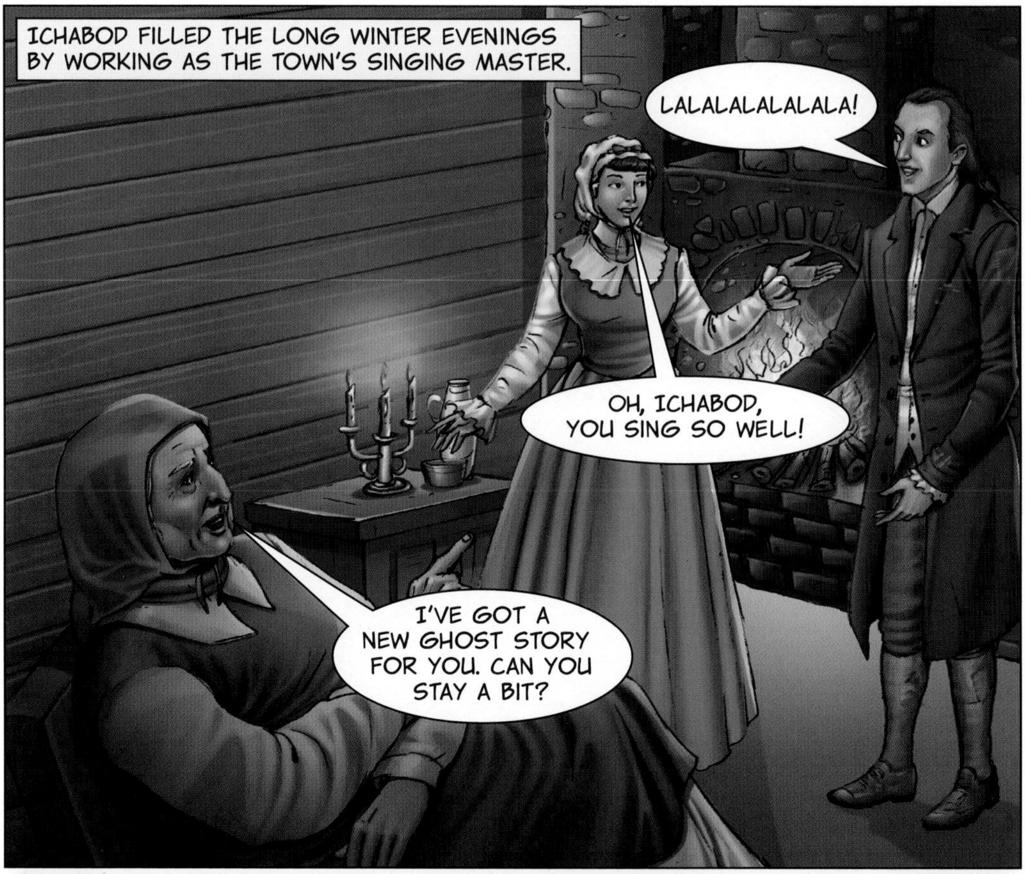
ICHABOD FILLED THE LONG WINTER EVENINGS BY WORKING AS THE TOWN'S SINGING MASTER.
LALALALALALALA!
OH, ICHABOD, YOU SING SO WELL!
I'VE GOT A NEW GHOST STORY FOR YOU. CAN YOU STAY A BIT?

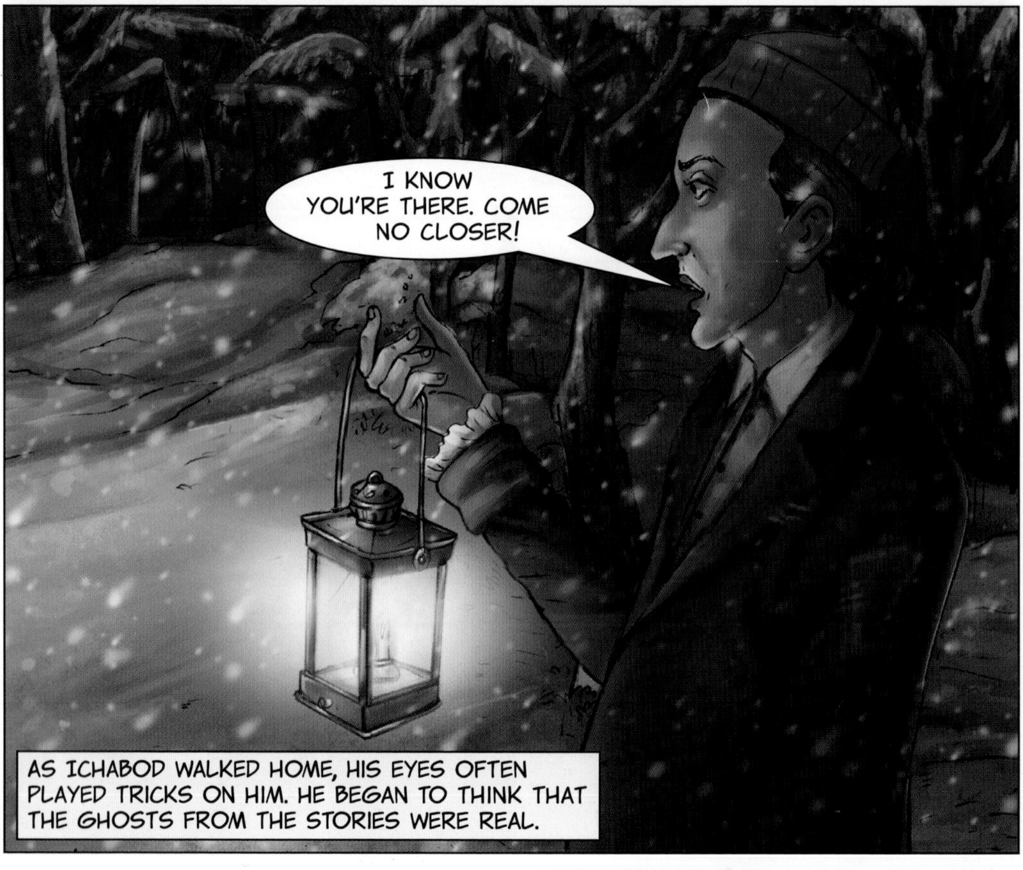
I KNOW YOU'RE THERE. COME NO CLOSER!
AS ICHABOD WALKED HOME, HIS EYES OFTEN PLAYED TRICKS ON HIM. HE BEGAN TO THINK THAT THE GHOSTS FROM THE STORIES WERE REAL.

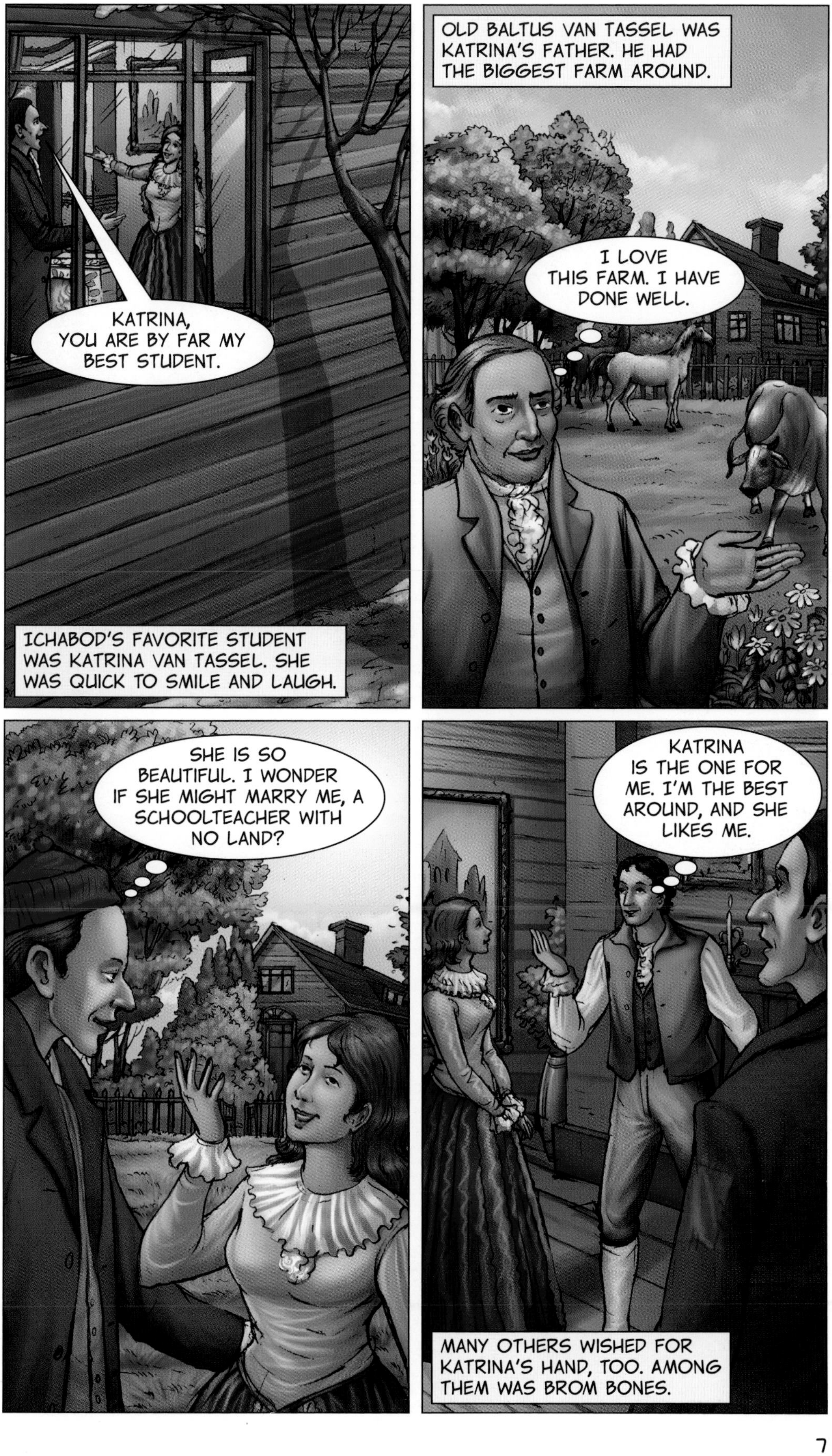
KATRINA, YOU ARE BY FAR MY BEST STUDENT.
ICHABOD'S FAVORITE STUDENT WAS KATRINA VAN TASSEL. SHE WAS QUICK TO SMILE AND LAUGH.
OLD BALTUS VAN TASSEL WAS KATRINA'S FATHER. HE HAD THE BIGGEST FARM AROUND.
I LOVE THIS FARM. I HAVE DONE WELL.
SHE IS SO BEAUTIFUL. I WONDER IF SHE MIGHT MARRY ME, A SCHOOLTEACHER WITH NO LAND?
KATRINA IS THE ONE FOR ME. I'M THE BEST AROUND, AND SHE LIKES ME.
MANY OTHERS WISHED FOR KATRINA'S HAND, TOO. AMONG THEM WAS BROM BONES.

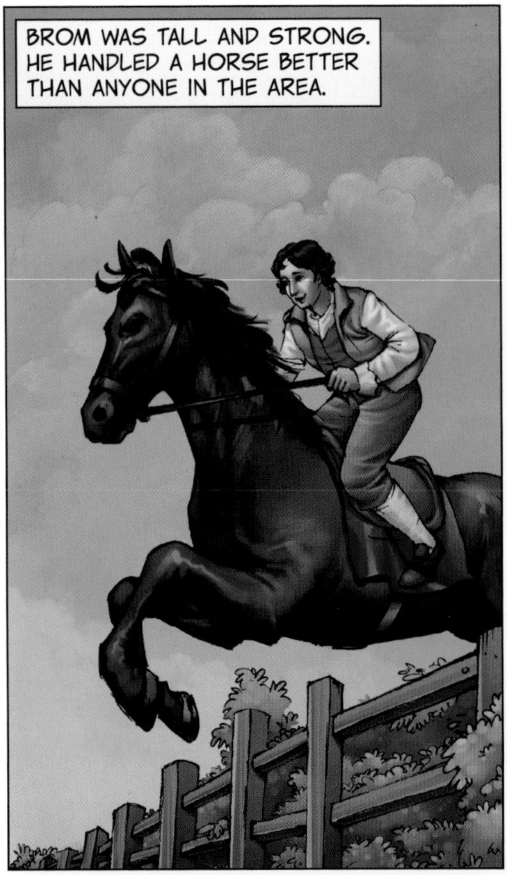
BROM WAS TALL AND STRONG. HE HANDLED A HORSE BETTER THAN ANYONE IN THE AREA.

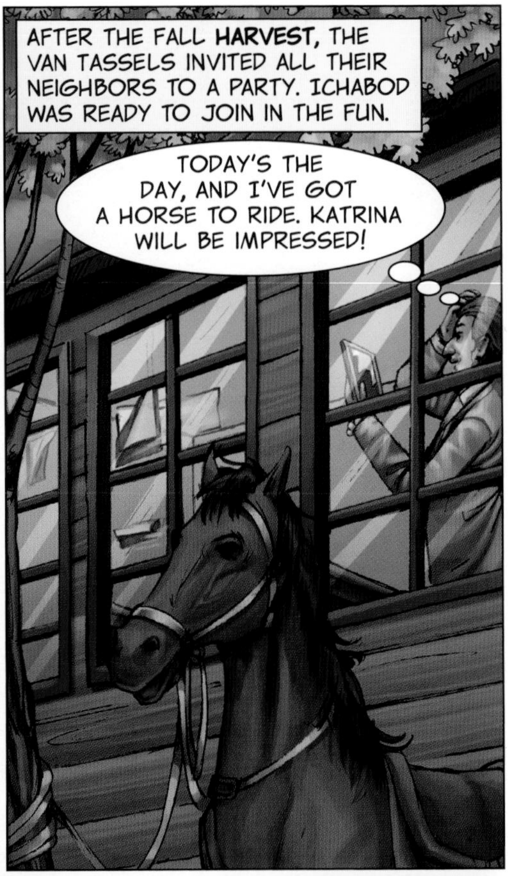
AFTER THE FALL **HARVEST,** THE VAN TASSELS INVITED ALL THEIR NEIGHBORS TO A PARTY. ICHABOD WAS READY TO JOIN IN THE FUN.
TODAY'S THE DAY, AND I'VE GOT A HORSE TO RIDE. KATRINA WILL BE IMPRESSED!

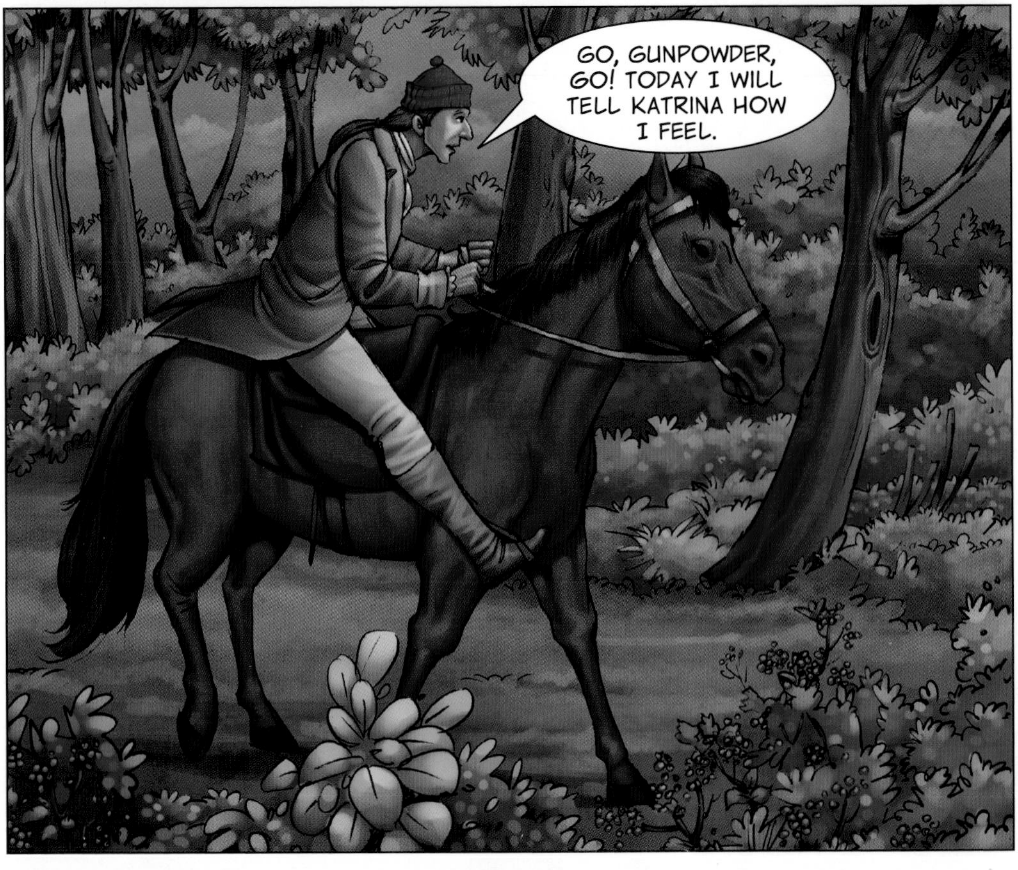
GO, GUNPOWDER, GO! TODAY I WILL TELL KATRINA HOW I FEEL.

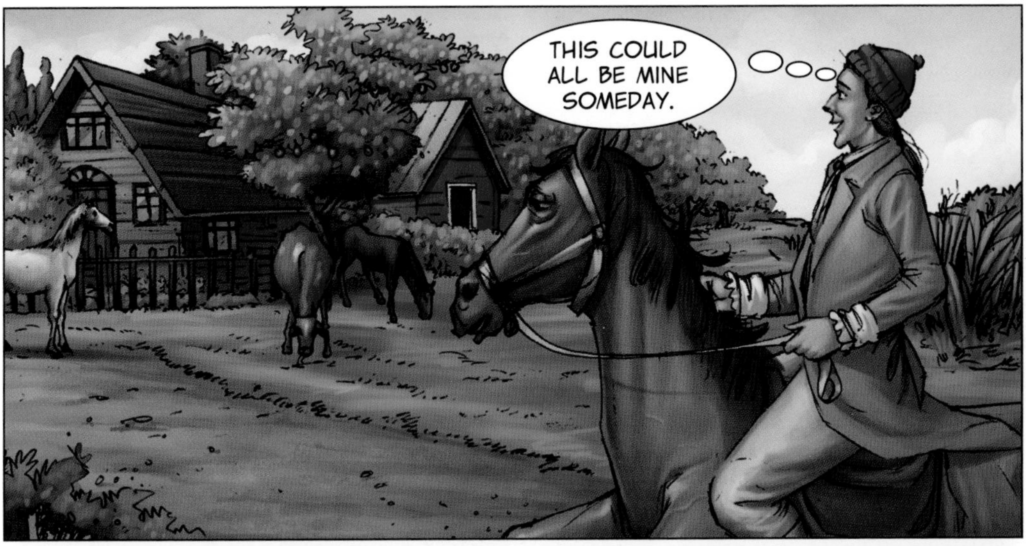
THIS COULD ALL BE MINE SOMEDAY.

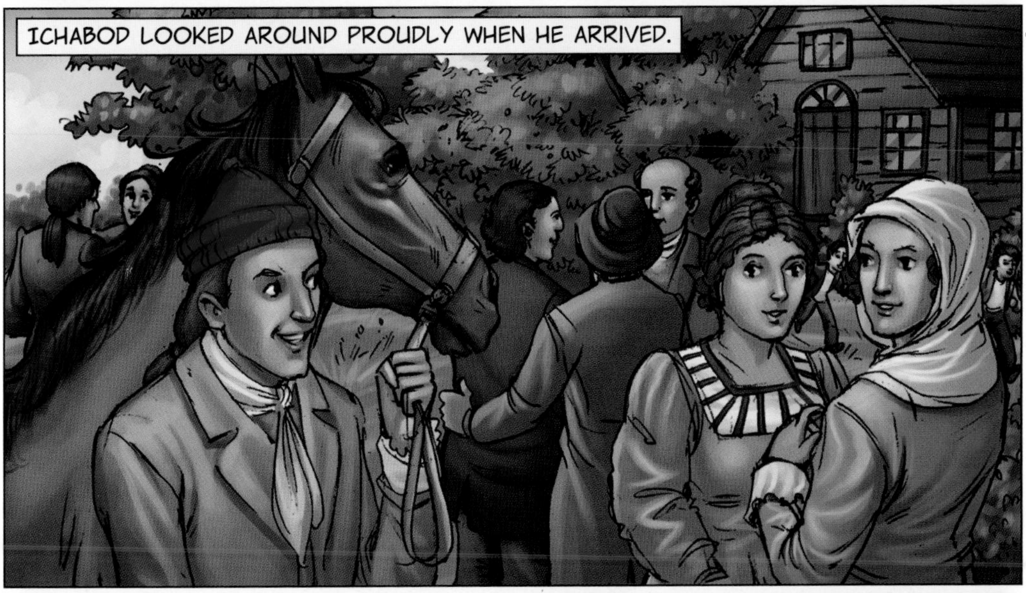
ICHABOD LOOKED AROUND PROUDLY WHEN HE ARRIVED.

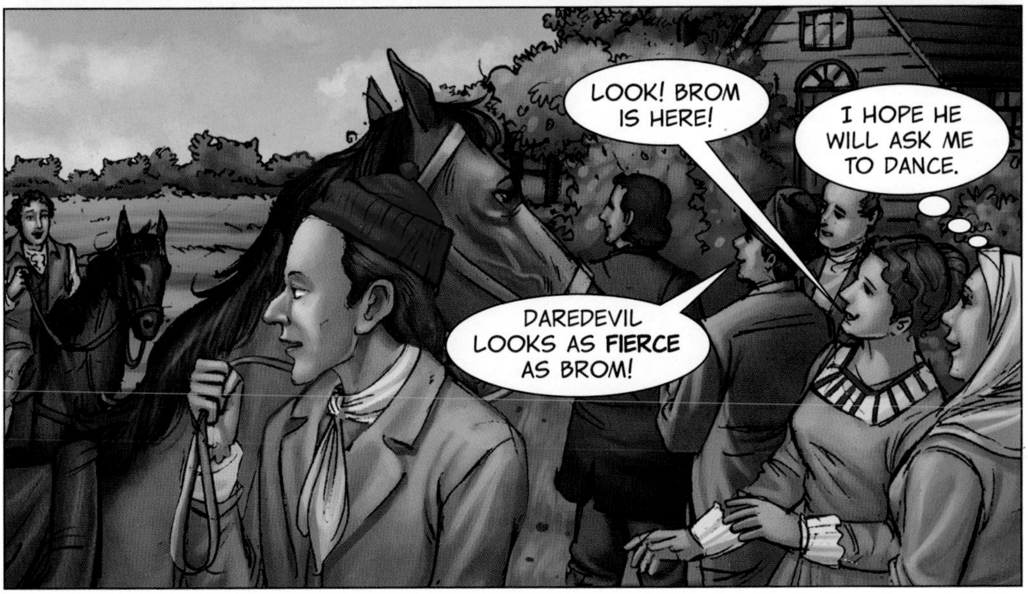
LOOK! BROM IS HERE!
I HOPE HE WILL ASK ME TO DANCE.
DAREDEVIL LOOKS AS **FIERCE** AS BROM!

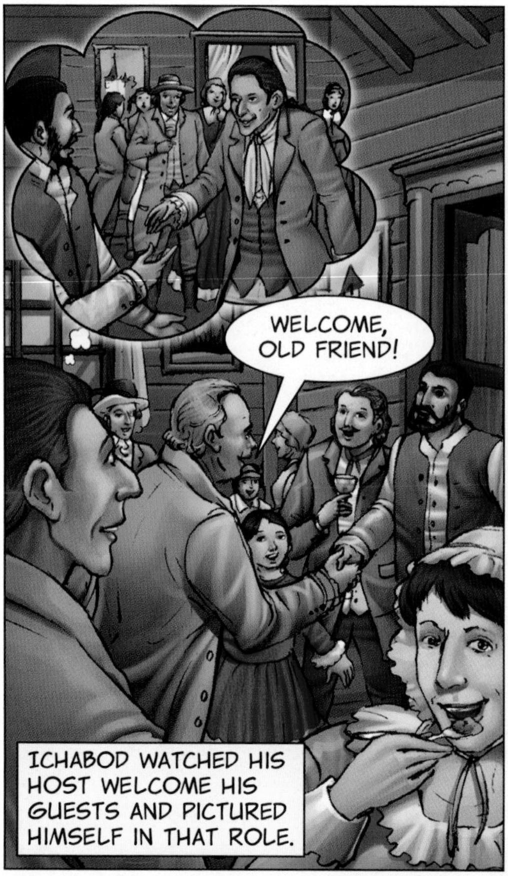
WELCOME, OLD FRIEND!
ICHABOD WATCHED HIS HOST WELCOME HIS GUESTS AND PICTURED HIMSELF IN THAT ROLE.

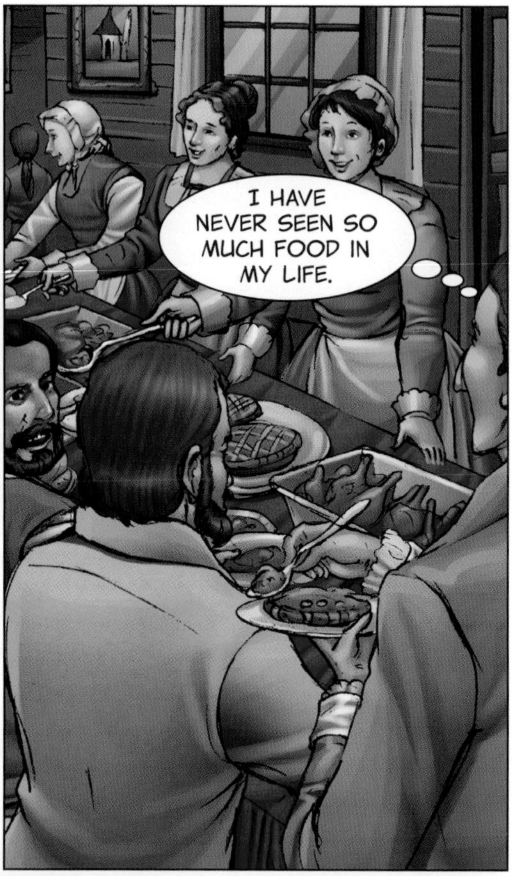
I HAVE NEVER SEEN SO MUCH FOOD IN MY LIFE.

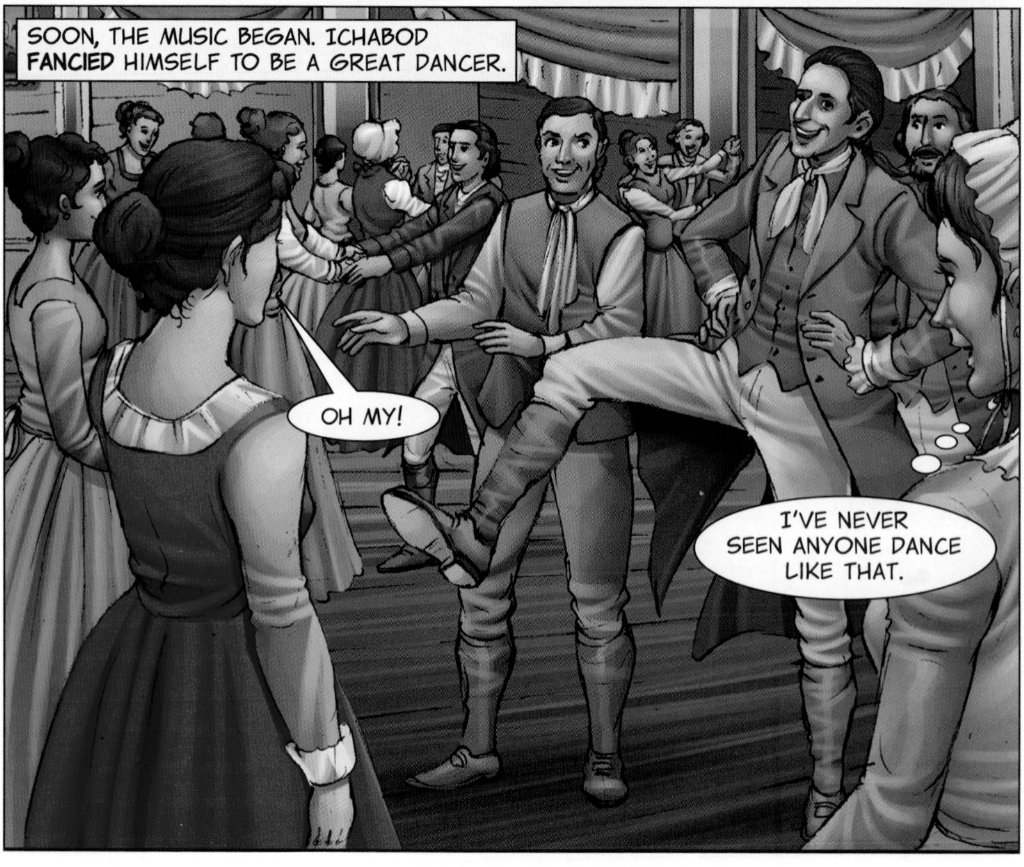
SOON, THE MUSIC BEGAN. ICHABOD **FANCIED** HIMSELF TO BE A GREAT DANCER.
OH MY!
I'VE NEVER SEEN ANYONE DANCE LIKE THAT.

AT NIGHTFALL, THE MEN BEGAN SHARING GHOST STORIES.

AS THE VISITOR NEARED THE GREAT TREE, HE WAS MET WITH MOANING THAT COULD ONLY HAVE COME FROM A GHOST.

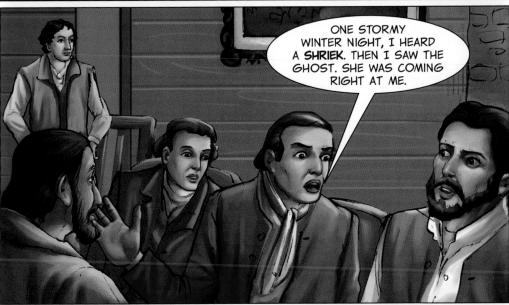

ONE STORMY WINTER NIGHT, I HEARD A **SHRIEK**. THEN I SAW THE GHOST. SHE WAS COMING RIGHT AT ME.

AS THE PARTY ENDED, ONE OF THE MEN SHARED THE LAST STORY. IT WAS BY FAR THE SCARIEST.

AS THE HEADLESS HORSEMAN REACHED THE BRIDGE, HE **VANISHED** IN A **BOLT** OF FLAMES.

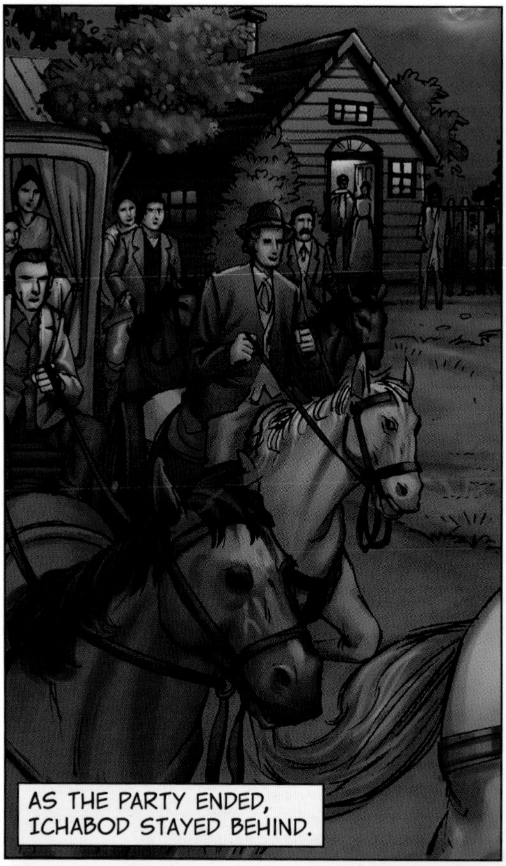
AS THE PARTY ENDED, ICHABOD STAYED BEHIND.

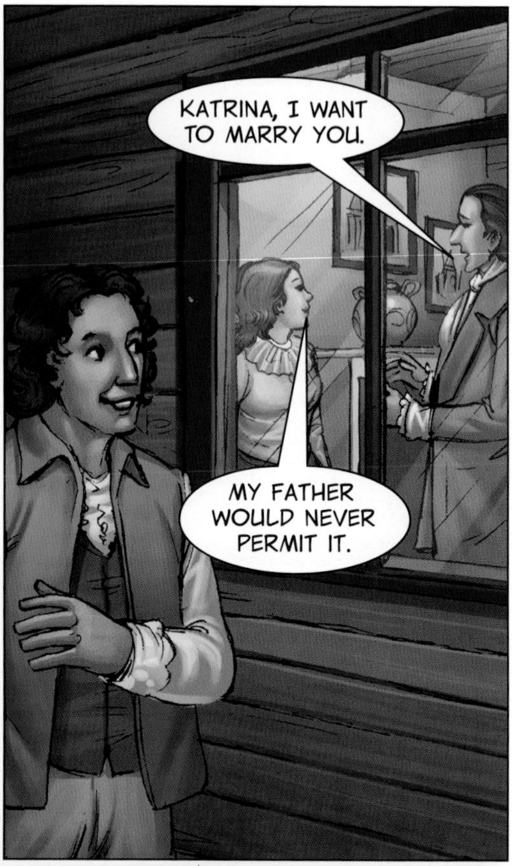
KATRINA, I WANT TO MARRY YOU.
MY FATHER WOULD NEVER PERMIT IT.

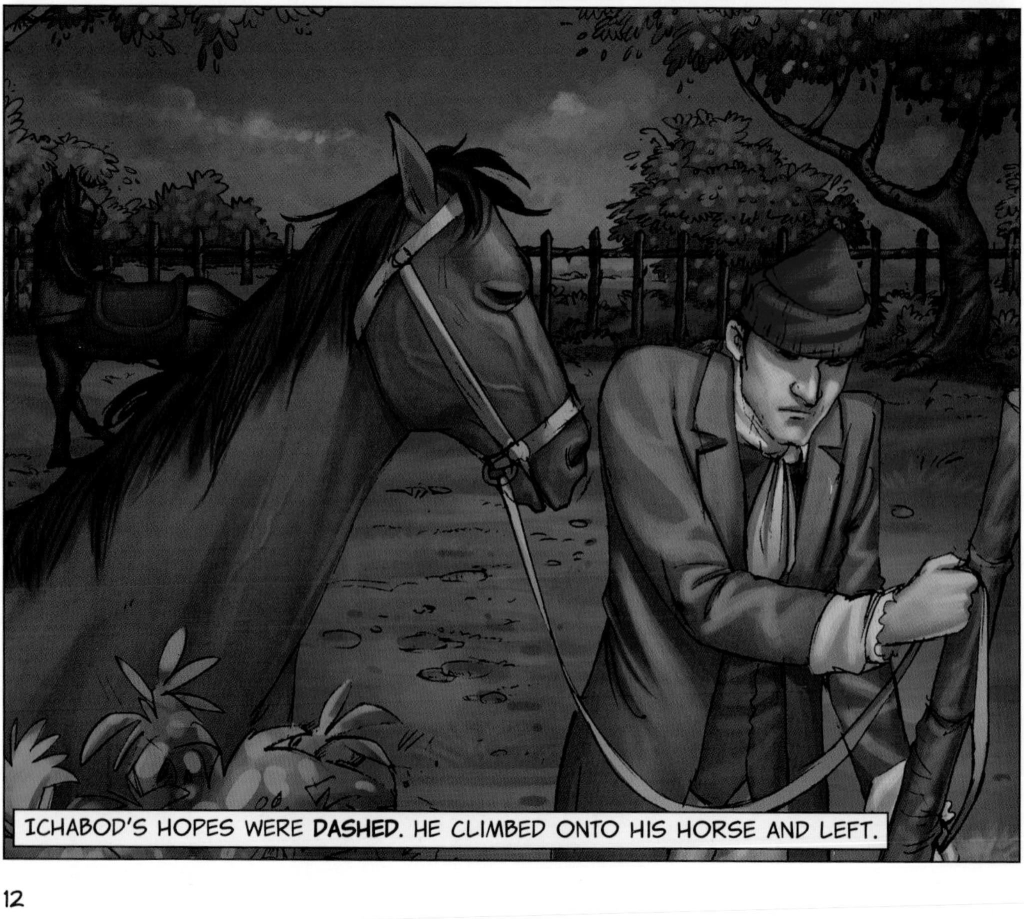
ICHABOD'S HOPES WERE **DASHED**. HE CLIMBED ONTO HIS HORSE AND LEFT.

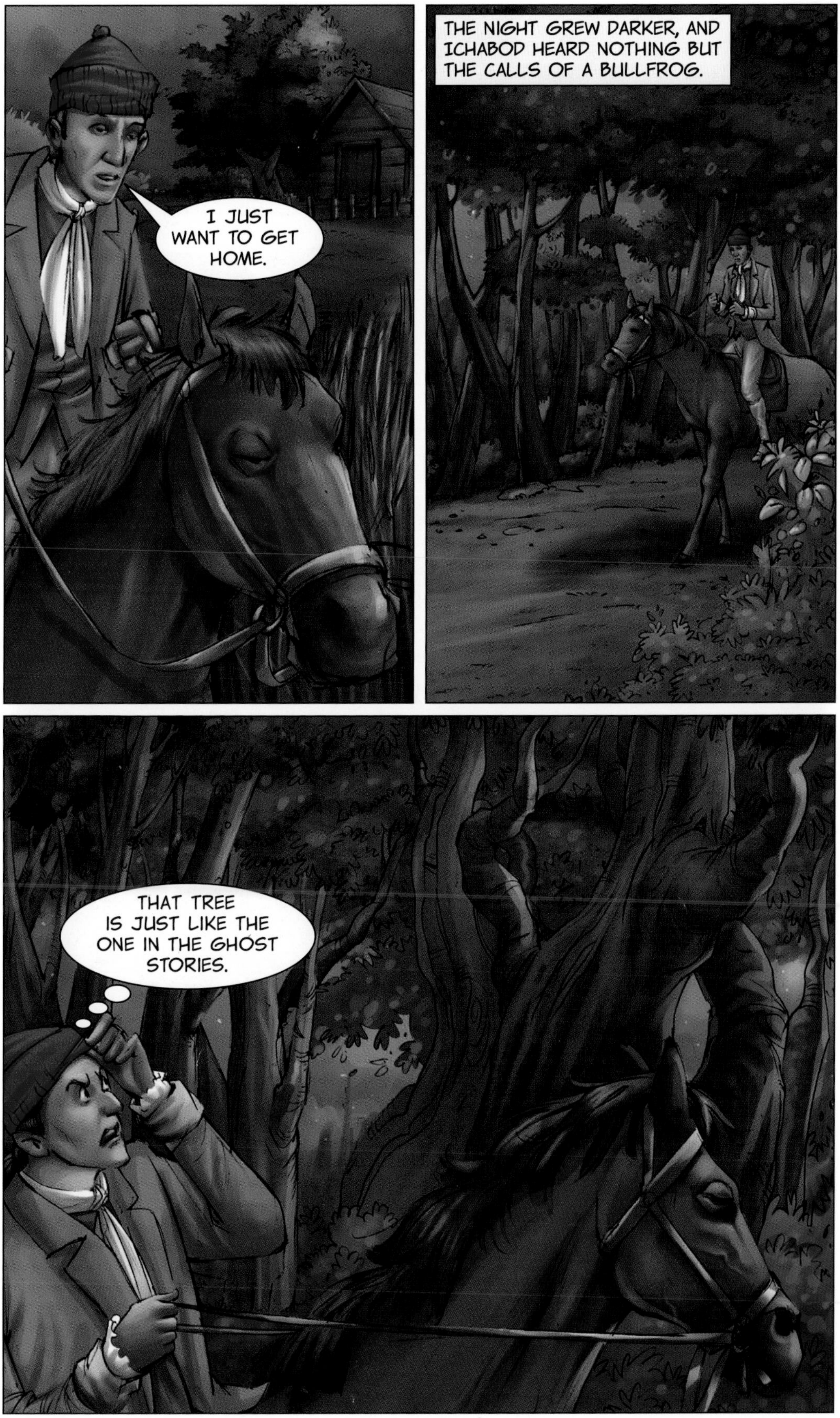
I JUST WANT TO GET HOME.
THE NIGHT GREW DARKER, AND ICHABOD HEARD NOTHING BUT THE CALLS OF A BULLFROG.
THAT TREE IS JUST LIKE THE ONE IN THE GHOST STORIES.

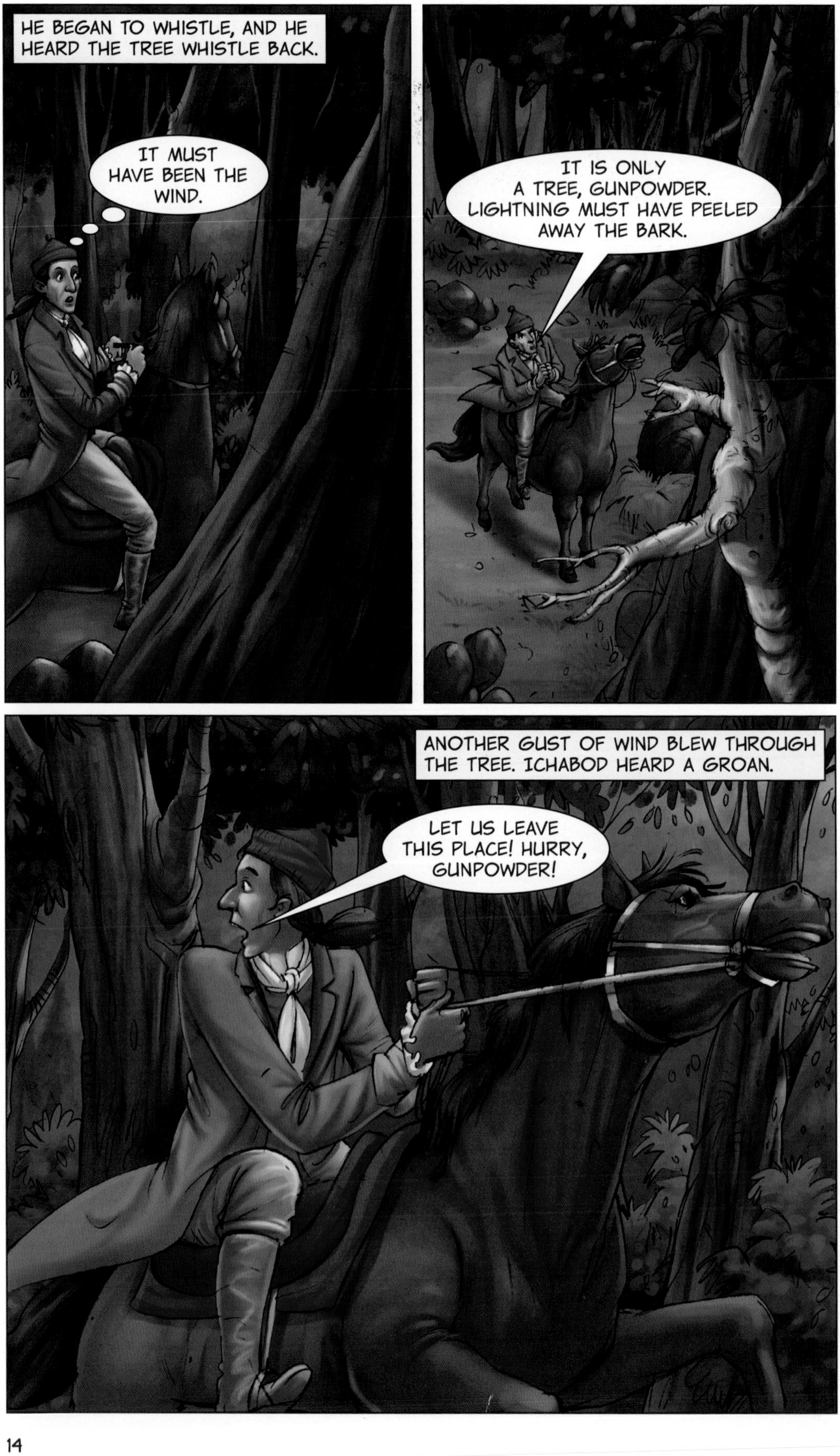
HE BEGAN TO WHISTLE, AND HE HEARD THE TREE WHISTLE BACK.
IT MUST HAVE BEEN THE WIND.
IT IS ONLY A TREE, GUNPOWDER. LIGHTNING MUST HAVE PEELED AWAY THE BARK.
ANOTHER GUST OF WIND BLEW THROUGH THE TREE. ICHABOD HEARD A GROAN.
LET US LEAVE THIS PLACE! HURRY, GUNPOWDER!

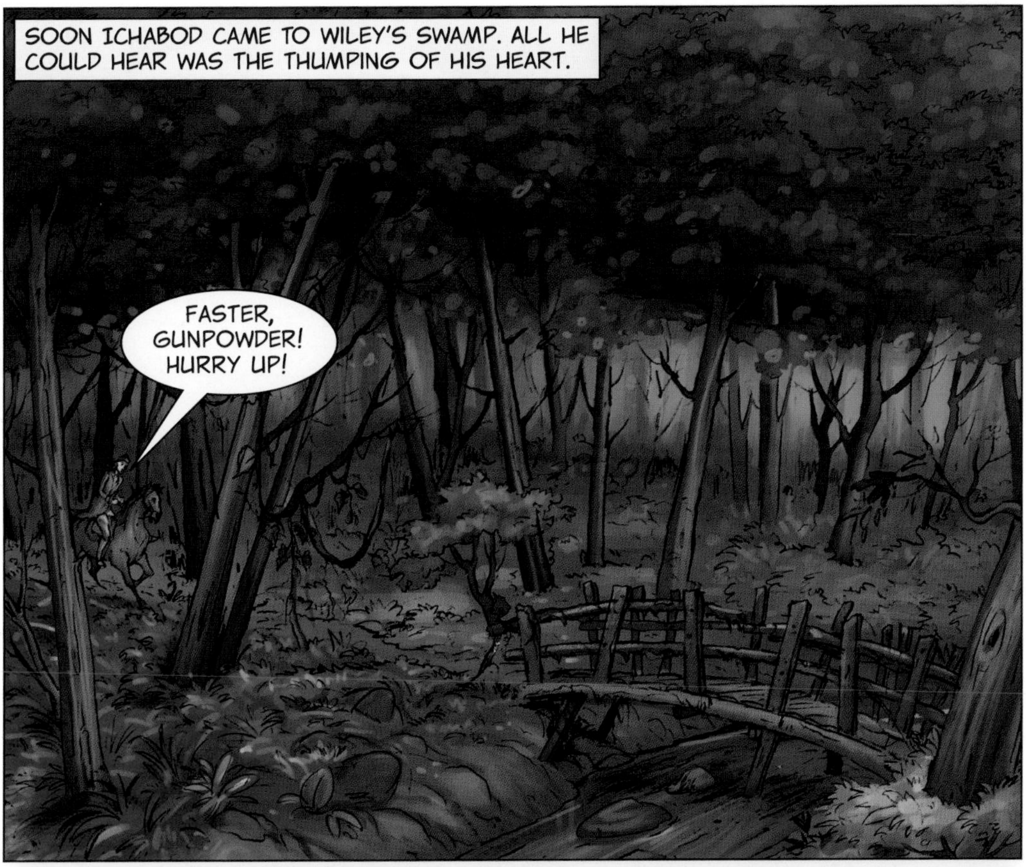
SOON ICHABOD CAME TO WILEY'S SWAMP. ALL HE COULD HEAR WAS THE THUMPING OF HIS HEART.
FASTER, GUNPOWDER! HURRY UP!

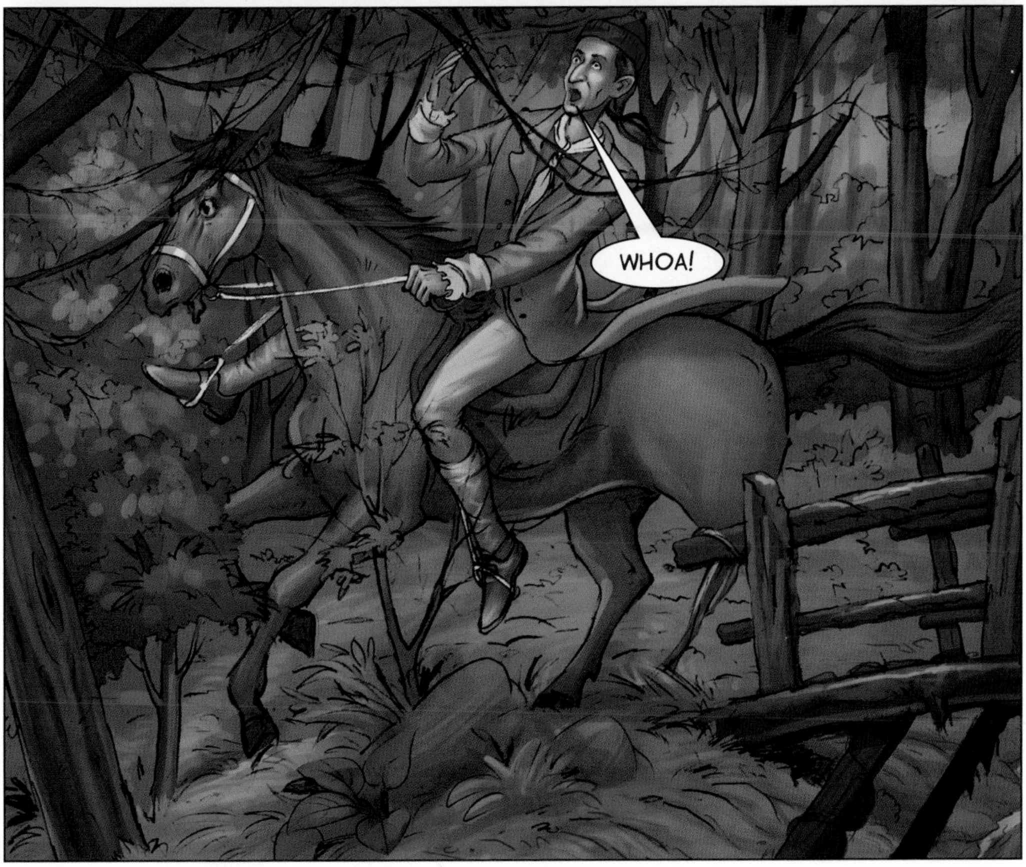
WHOA!

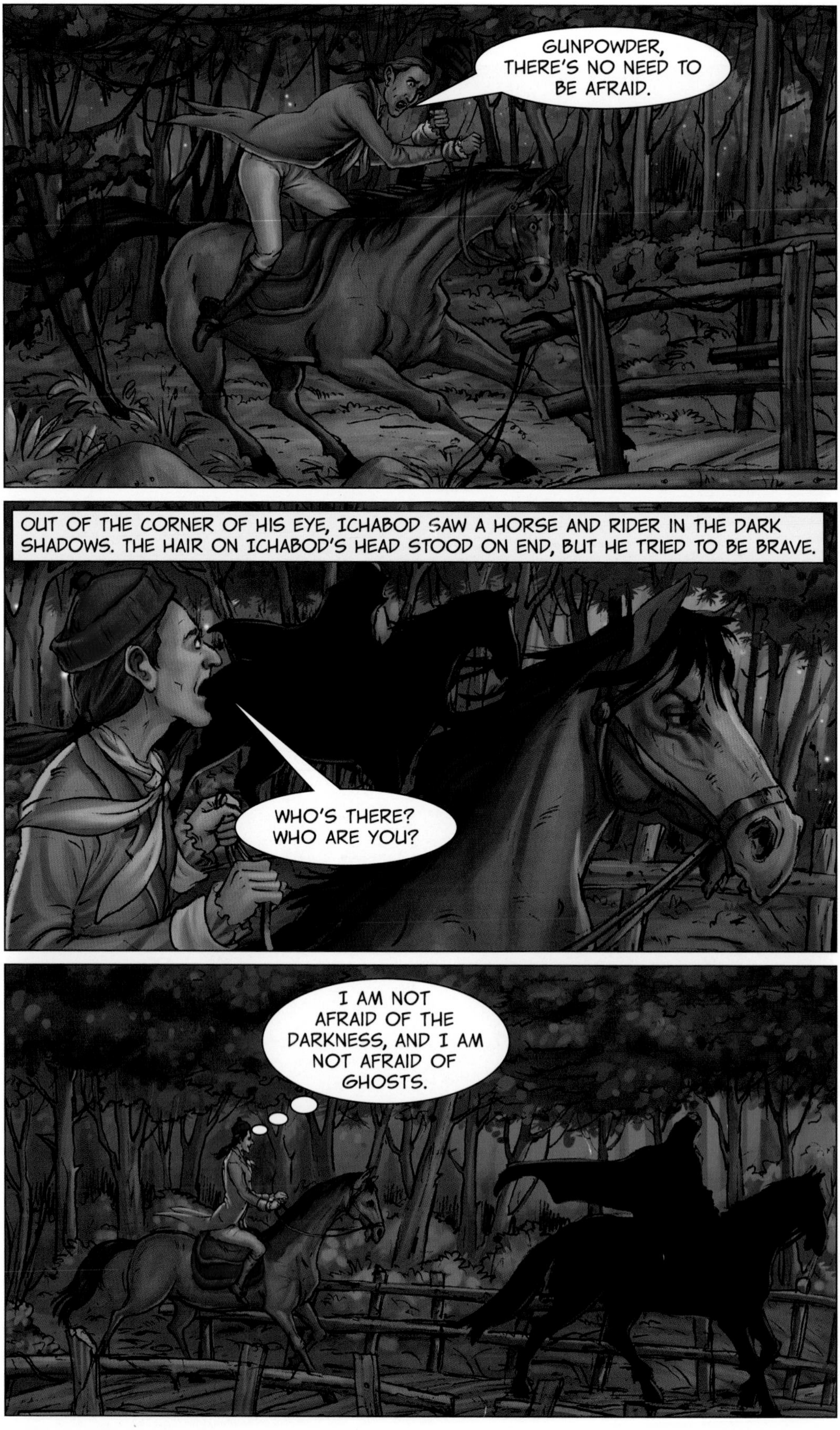
GUNPOWDER, THERE'S NO NEED TO BE AFRAID.
OUT OF THE CORNER OF HIS EYE, ICHABOD SAW A HORSE AND RIDER IN THE DARK SHADOWS. THE HAIR ON ICHABOD'S HEAD STOOD ON END, BUT HE TRIED TO BE BRAVE.
WHO'S THERE? WHO ARE YOU?
I AM NOT AFRAID OF THE DARKNESS, AND I AM NOT AFRAID OF GHOSTS.

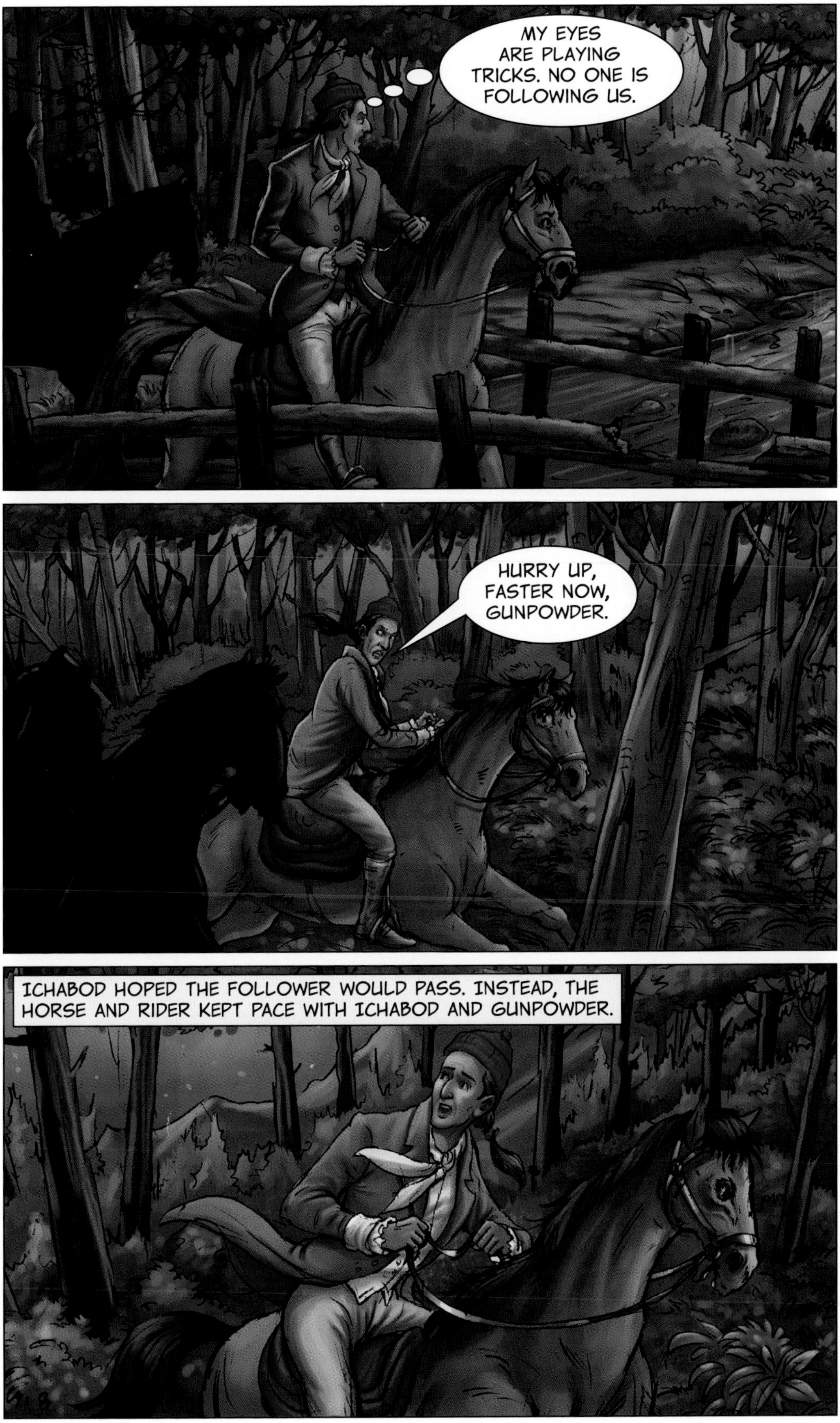
MY EYES ARE PLAYING TRICKS. NO ONE IS FOLLOWING US.
HURRY UP, FASTER NOW, GUNPOWDER.
ICHABOD HOPED THE FOLLOWER WOULD PASS. INSTEAD, THE HORSE AND RIDER KEPT PACE WITH ICHABOD AND GUNPOWDER.

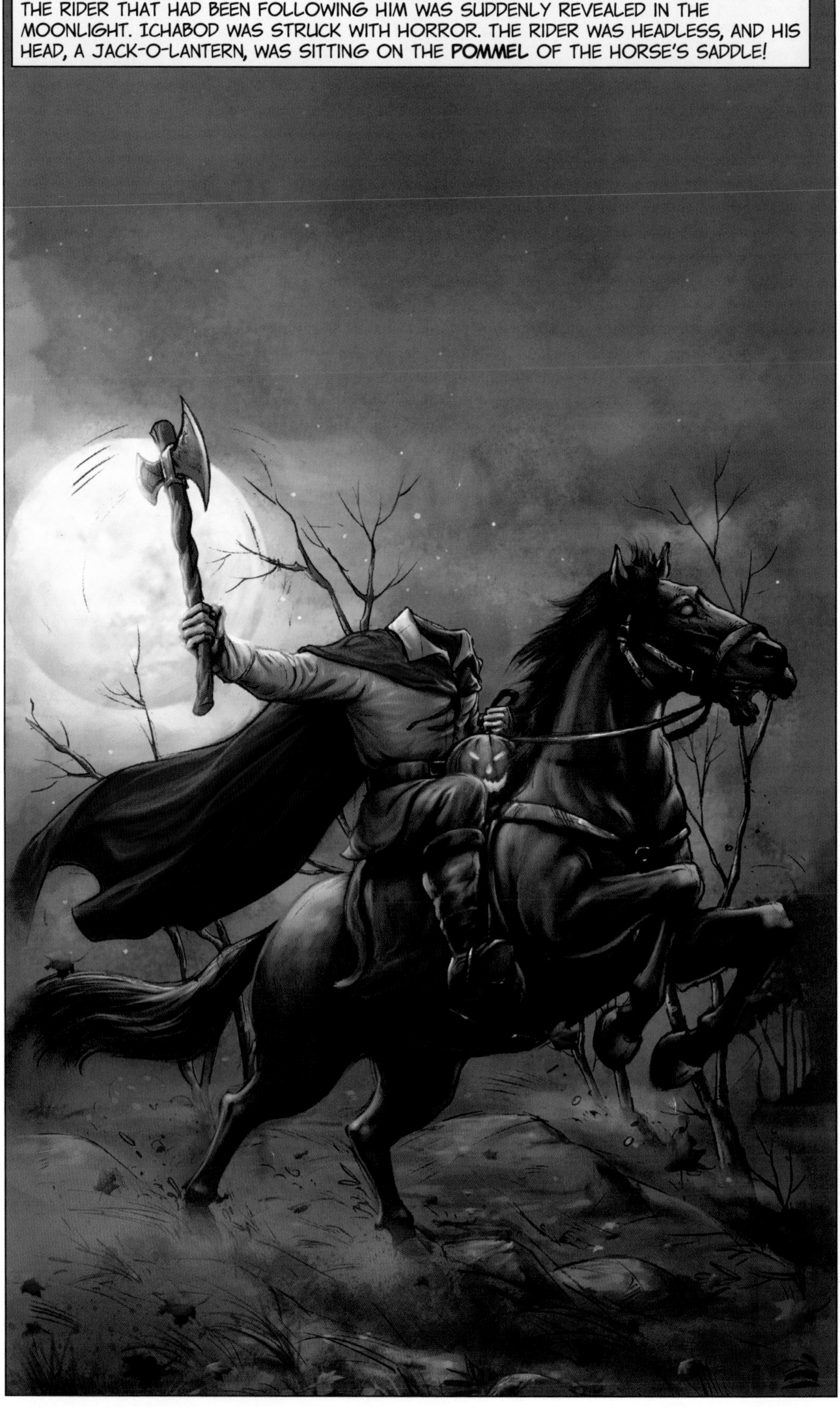
THE RIDER THAT HAD BEEN FOLLOWING HIM WAS SUDDENLY REVEALED IN THE MOONLIGHT. ICHABOD WAS STRUCK WITH HORROR. THE RIDER WAS HEADLESS, AND HIS HEAD, A JACK-O-LANTERN, WAS SITTING ON THE **POMMEL** OF THE HORSE'S SADDLE!

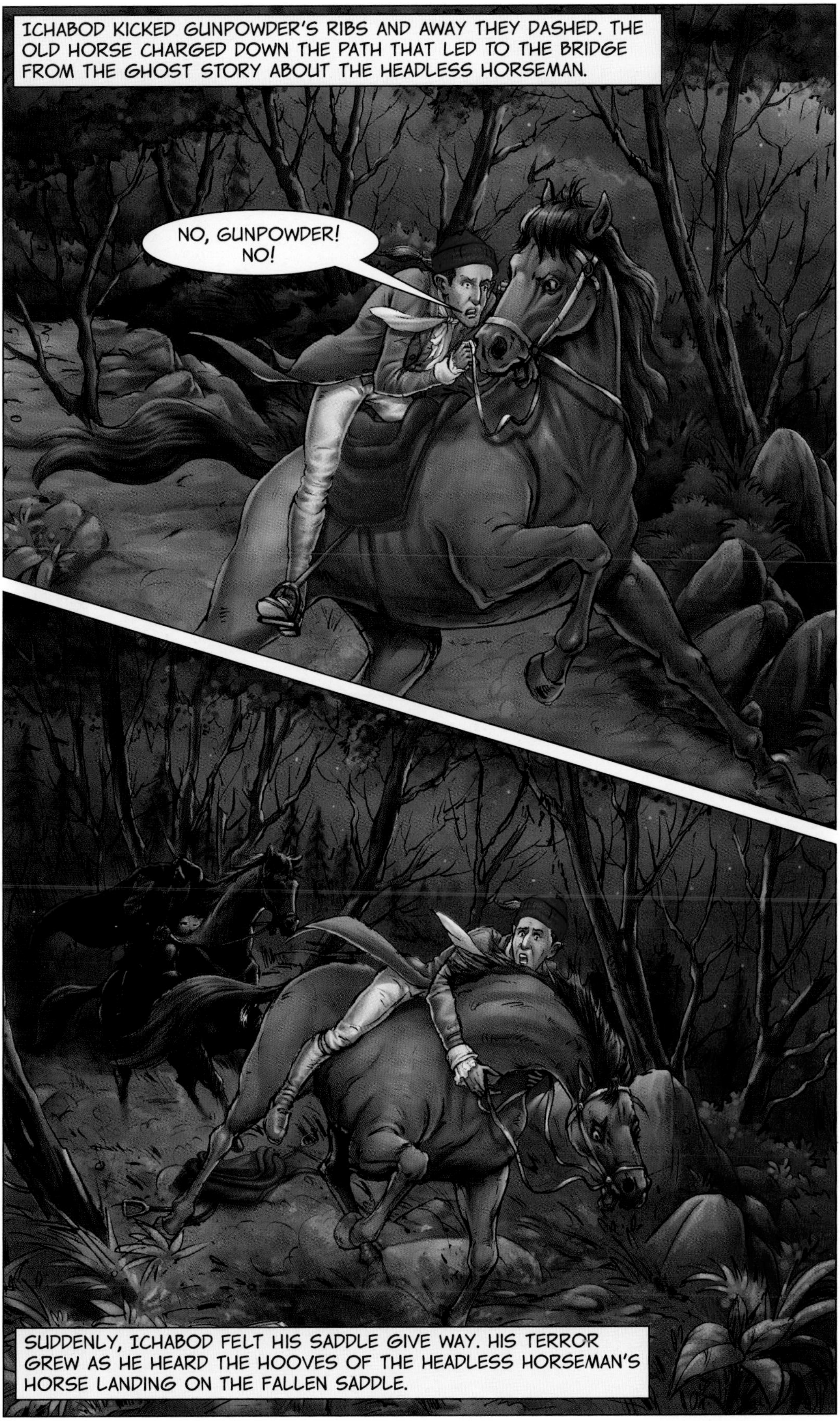
ICHABOD KICKED GUNPOWDER'S RIBS AND AWAY THEY DASHED. THE OLD HORSE CHARGED DOWN THE PATH THAT LED TO THE BRIDGE FROM THE GHOST STORY ABOUT THE HEADLESS HORSEMAN.
NO, GUNPOWDER! NO!
SUDDENLY, ICHABOD FELT HIS SADDLE GIVE WAY. HIS TERROR GREW AS HE HEARD THE HOOVES OF THE HEADLESS HORSEMAN'S HORSE LANDING ON THE FALLEN SADDLE.

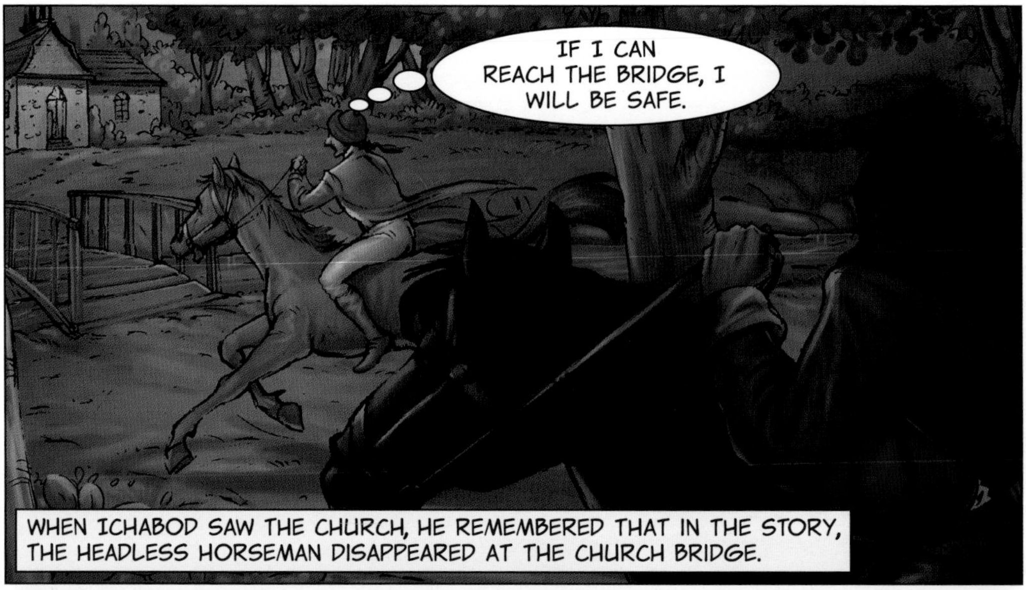
IF I CAN REACH THE BRIDGE, I WILL BE SAFE.
WHEN ICHABOD SAW THE CHURCH, HE REMEMBERED THAT IN THE STORY, THE HEADLESS HORSEMAN DISAPPEARED AT THE CHURCH BRIDGE.

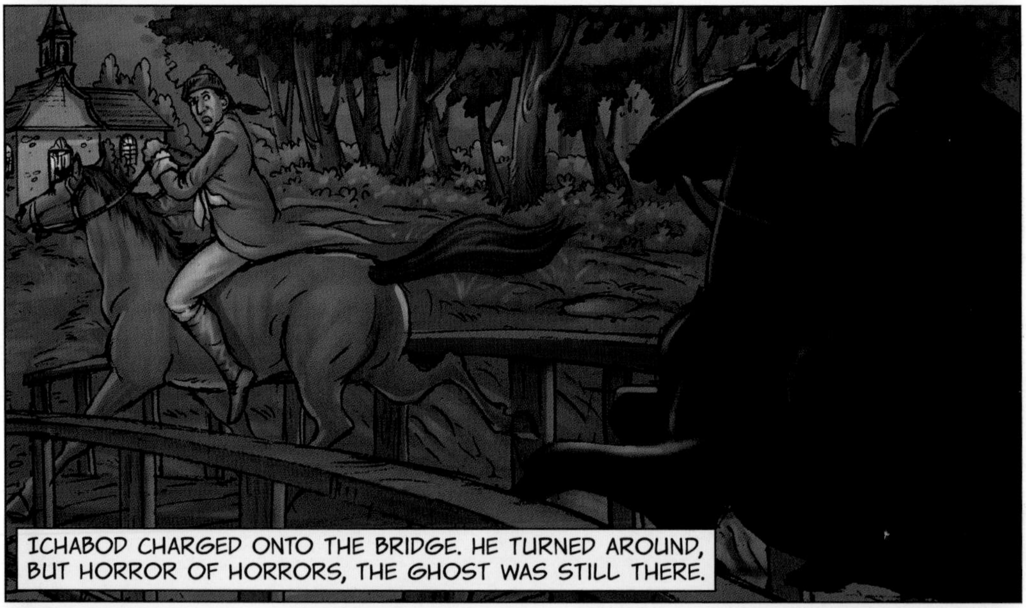
ICHABOD CHARGED ONTO THE BRIDGE. HE TURNED AROUND, BUT HORROR OF HORRORS, THE GHOST WAS STILL THERE.

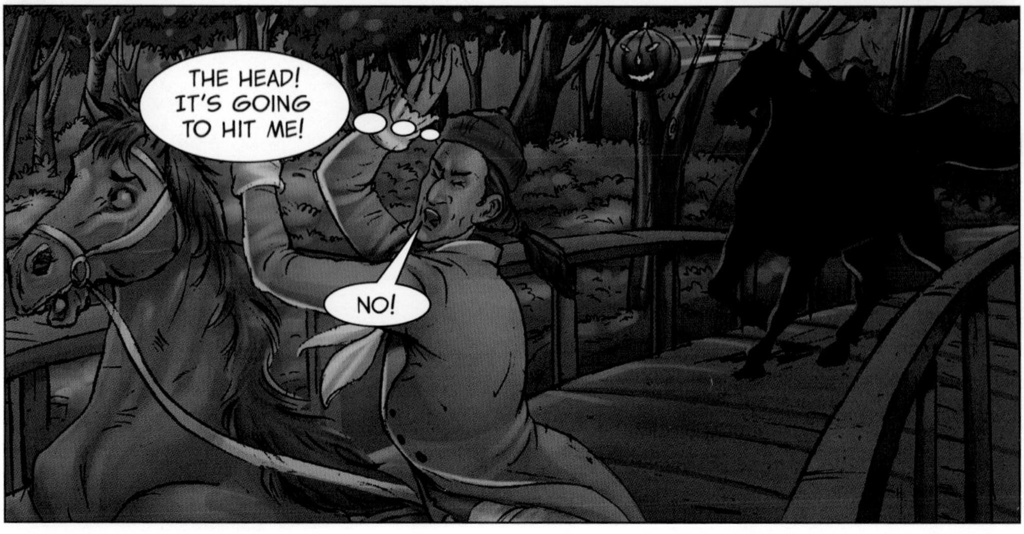
THE HEAD! IT'S GOING TO HIT ME!
NO!

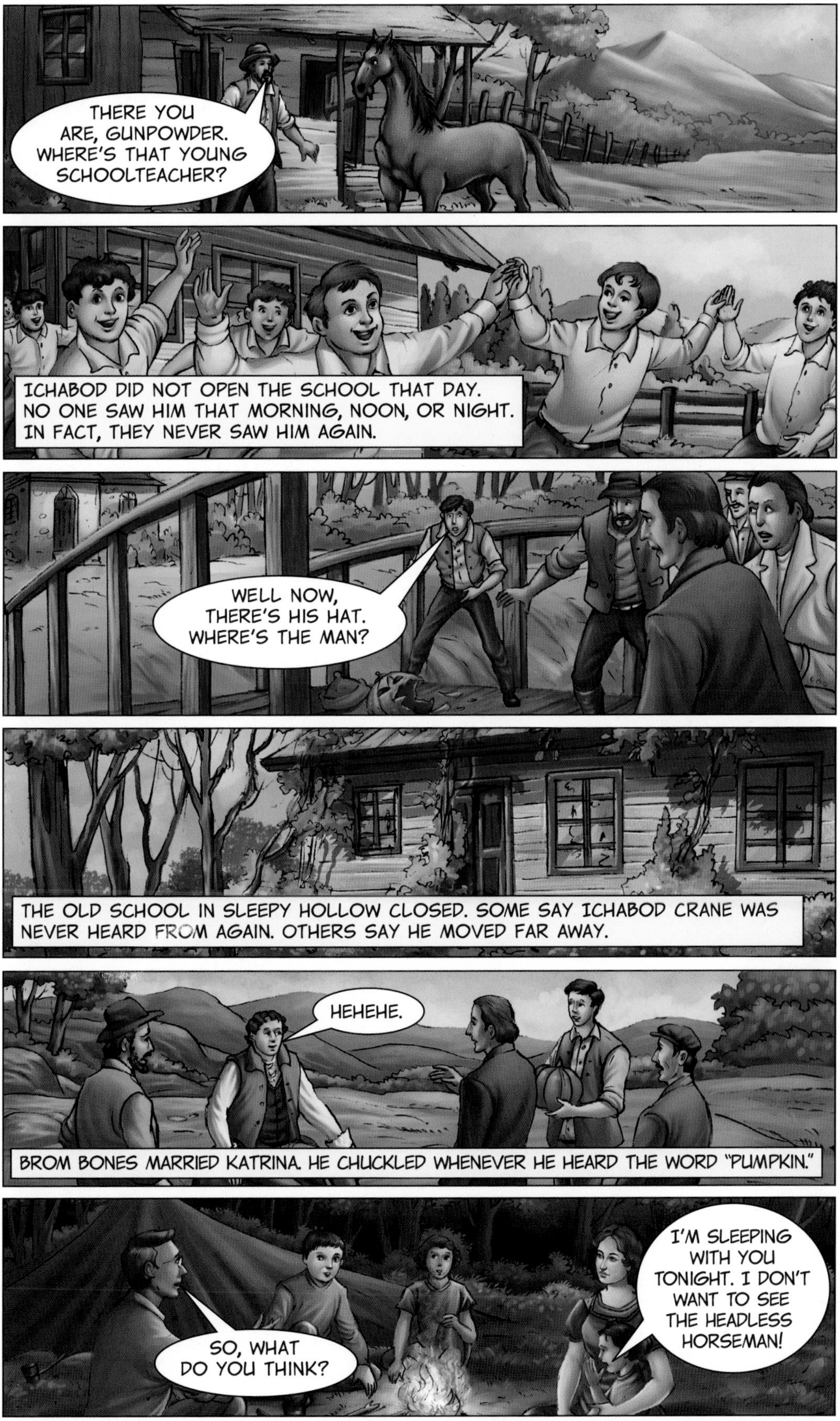
THERE YOU ARE, GUNPOWDER. WHERE'S THAT YOUNG SCHOOLTEACHER?
ICHABOD DID NOT OPEN THE SCHOOL THAT DAY. NO ONE SAW HIM THAT MORNING, NOON, OR NIGHT. IN FACT, THEY NEVER SAW HIM AGAIN.
WELL NOW, THERE'S HIS HAT. WHERE'S THE MAN?
THE OLD SCHOOL IN SLEEPY HOLLOW CLOSED. SOME SAY ICHABOD CRANE WAS NEVER HEARD FROM AGAIN. OTHERS SAY HE MOVED FAR AWAY.
HEHEHE.
BROM BONES MARRIED KATRINA. HE CHUCKLED WHENEVER HE HEARD THE WORD "PUMPKIN."
SO, WHAT DO YOU THINK?
I'M SLEEPING WITH YOU TONIGHT. I DON'T WANT TO SEE THE HEADLESS HORSEMAN!

More Ghost Stories

- **The Lady in White of Raven Rock** is the story of a young girl who lost her way in a snowstorm. She tried to find shelter from the wind by staying by the rock pile called Raven Rock. The girl never made it home. The legend says her ghost wanders Buttermilk Hill in snowstorms. Her cries sound like the howling wind and warn others to stay away from Raven Rock.

- **The Ghost of Major André** is said to ride through Patriot's Park, a place not far from Sleepy Hollow. André was a British spy during the American Revolution. He was captured and hanged on a spot where the park now stands.

- **Old Leather Man** is the story of Dead Man's Cave in Saw Mill Woods, New York. It is said that an old vagrant, who dressed completely in leather, hid his treasure in a cave there. In the late 1800s, a farmer went into the cave to find the treasure. Instead, he found the ghost of Old Leather Man. The ghost blew out the farmer's light and chased him from the cave.

- **Widow's Watch of Rondout Lighthouse** is the story of the ghost of a young widow. The young bride's husband was the **lighthouse** keeper. On their wedding day, the husband was lost at sea. It is said that the young bride's ghost roams the lighthouse every night searching for her lost husband.

- **The Ghost of Dolley Madison** is the story of the former first lady. Dolley Madison had a rose garden planted on the White House grounds while her husband, James Madison, was president. It is said her ghost still roams the garden and protects it from being disturbed.

Glossary

bolt (BOLT) A stroke, like that of lightning.

dashed (DASHD) Broken or destroyed.

fancied (FANT-seed) Believed mistakenly.

fierce (FEERS) Strong and ready to fight.

glens (GLENZ) Small valleys usually covered with grass.

harvest (HAR-vist) The gathering of the season's crops.

Hessian (HEH-shen) A German soldier who was paid to fight for the British during the American Revolution.

legend (LEH-jend) A story, passed down through the years, that cannot be proved.

lighthouse (LYT-hows) A tall structure built near the shore with a powerful light on the top used to guide ships away from danger.

pommel (PUH-mul) The raised, rounded part on the front of a saddle.

shriek (SHREEK) A loud, high-pitched cry.

singing master (SING-ing MA-ster) A man who teaches singing.

vanished (VA-nishd) Disappeared mysteriously.

Index

A
American Revolution, 3, 22
André, Major, 22

B
Bones, Brom, 3, 7, 8, 9, 21
Buttermilk Hill, 22

H
Headless Horseman, 3, 5, 11,
    19, 20
Hessian, 3
Hudson River, 4

I
Irving, Washington, 3, 4, 5

M
Madison, Dolley, 22

N
New York, 3, 22

O
Old Dutch Church, 4, 20
Old Leather Man, 22

P
Patriot's Park, 22

R
Raven Rock, 22
Rondout Lighthouse, 22

S
Saw Mill Woods, 22
singing master, 3, 6
Sleepy Hollow, 3, 4, 5, 21, 22

T
Tarrytown, 4

V
Van Tassel, Baltus, 3, 7, 8
Van Tassel, Katrina, 3, 7, 8,
    12, 21

W
White House, 22
Wiley's Swamp, 15

Websites

Due to the changing nature of Internet links, PowerKids Press has developed an online list of websites related to the subject of this book. This site is updated regularly. Please use this link to access the list:

www.powerkidslinks.com/jggs/sleepy/